BRAZIL

Many Voices, Many Faces

Caribbean Sea

NORTH ATLANTIC OCEAN

VENEZUELA

COLOMBIA

GUYANA

SURINAME

FR. GUIANA

RORAIMA

Guiana Highlands

AMAPÁ

Equator

▲ Pico da Neblina
(9,889 ft / 3,014 m)

Amazon River

Marajó Island

● Belém

Manaus ●

Amazon Basin

PARÁ

MARANHÃO

CEARÁ

RIO GRANDE DO NORTE

● Natal

AMAZONAS

PIAUÍ

Pombal ●

PARAÍBA

● Olinda
Recife

ACRE

PERNAMBUCO

ALAGOAS

RONDÔNIA

TOCANTINS

São Francísco River

SERGIPE

PERU

MATO GROSSO

BAHIA

● Salvador

BOLIVIA

Paraguay River

Brasília
FEDERAL DISTRICT

Central Highlands

GOIÁS

MINAS GERAIS

MATO GROSSO DO SUL

ESPÍRITO SANTO

Ouro Prêto ●

SÃO PAULO

São Paulo ●

RIO DE JANEIRO

PARAGUAY

PARANÁ

Iguaçú Falls

Rio de Janeiro ●

Tropic of Capricorn

SOUTH PACIFIC OCEAN

CHILE

A R G E N T I N A

SANTA CATARINA

RIO GRANDE DO SUL

Pôrto Alegre ●

URUGUAY

SOUTH ATLANTIC OCEAN

Capital city
Major town
▲ Mountain peak

Feet	Meters
16,000	4,880
10,000	3,050
6,000	1,830
3,000	910
1,500	460
600	180
0	0

BRAZIL

N

0   200   400   600 Miles
0   200 400 600 800 Kilometers

© Oxford Cartographers

EXPLORING CULTURES OF THE WORLD

BRAZIL

Many Voices, Many Faces

Irene Flum Galvin

BENCHMARK BOOKS

MARSHALL CAVENDISH
NEW YORK

With thanks to Dr. Miriam Ayres,
Lecturer, Department of Spanish and Portuguese, New York University,
for her expert reading of the manuscript and
help above and beyond the call of duty in picture research.

Special thanks also to Sergio Tellaroli for his generous assistance.

TO THE CHILDREN OF BRAZIL

Benchmark Books
Marshall Cavendish Corporation
99 White Plains Road
Tarrytown, New York 10591-9001

© Marshall Cavendish Corporation 1996

Library of Congress Cataloging-in-Publication Data

Galvin, Irene Flum.
    Brazil : many voices, many faces / by Irene Flum Galvin.
       p.   cm. — (Exploring cultures of the world)
    Includes bibliographical references (p.   ).
    ISBN 0-7614-0200-4 (lib. bdg.)
    1. Brazil—Juvenile literature.   I. Title   II. Series.
  F2508.5.G35   1996
  981—dc20
                                                            95-44087

SUMMARY: Reviews the history, geography, people, customs, and the arts of Brazil.

Printed and bound in the U.S.A.

Book design by Carol Matsuyama
Photo research by Sandy Jones

Front cover: Carnival in Rio de Janeiro
Back cover: The 125-foot (38-meter)-tall statue of Christ on Corcovado Mountain overlooks the city of Rio de Janeiro.

Photo Credits

Front cover and pages 30, 32, 46, 49: courtesy of Robert Fried Photography; back cover and pages 9, 17: courtesy of Manfred Gottschalk/Tom Stack & Associates; pages 3, 33: courtesy of Haroldo de Faria Castro/FPG International; page 6: The "Alferes Tiradentes" by J. Wasth Rodrigues from Museu Historico Nacional, Rio de Janeiro; pages 11, 12 *(left)*: Buddy Mays/TRAVEL STOCK; page 12 *(top)*: Larry Tacket/Tom Stack & Associates; page 12 *(bottom)*: Joe McDonald/Tom Stack & Associates; pages 14, 47, 52: Archive Photos; page 15: Scala/Art Resource, NY; page 18: Giraudon/Art Resource, NY; page 20: Archive Photos/Imapress; page 22: Wolfgang Kaehler; page 23: Reuters/Bettmann; pages 25, 38: Image Bank; page 27: Michael Moody/DDB Stock Photos; page 28: Spencer Grant/FPG International; page 29: J. C. Lozovet/Image Bank; pages 31, 57: Jeff Greenberg/Unicorn Stock Photos; pages 35 *(left)*, 35 *(right)*, 36, 44, 53: Ulrike Welsch; page 40: Carl Purcell/WORDS & PICTURES; page 42: Lawrence S. Burr; page 50: Mary Altier; page 55: Bridgeman/Art Resource, NY; page 56: John Lewisstage/Image Bank

Contents

Inspired by the American Revolution, Tiradentes led Brazil's fight for independence.

1

GEOGRAPHY AND HISTORY

Land of the Mighty Amazon

The Tooth Puller

On November 12, 1748, a child was born in a small town in Brazil. He was named Joaquim José da Silva Xavier, and no one took much notice of his birth. One day, however, he would become famous throughout the land as Tiradentes, the Tooth Puller.

When Tiradentes was born, Brazil was still a colony. It belonged to Portugal. But Tiradentes had a dream that would change Brazil's history. He dreamed of freedom and independence. And one day, although he would never know it, his dream would come true.

Early in his life, Tiradentes fell in love with reading, thanks to the education he received from his brother, a priest. When Tiradentes grew up, he worked at several trades. He was a physician, a merchant, and a soldier. After he became a dentist, he got his nickname, the Tooth Puller. But no matter what job he had, Tiradentes kept reading.

In those days, Brazil didn't have a university or a printing press. It wasn't easy for Tiradentes to get books. When he could, he read the works of French and American writers. They had exciting new ideas about freedom and democracy. It is said that Tiradentes carried with him copies of the constitutions of the thirteen original states of the

United States. The American Revolution in 1776 and the French Revolution in 1789 inspired him to form a group to overthrow Portuguese rule.

Poets, priests, physicians, lawyers, and military officers joined Tiradentes in plotting against the Portuguese. They planned to demand complete independence from Portugal. They also wanted to abolish slavery, help the poor, and—something dear to Tiradentes's heart—start a university. They created a flag with a symbol of their hopes—a picture of an Indian breaking his chains—and prepared to defend it with guns.

But before the first shot was fired, a spy told the Portuguese governor about their plans, and they were arrested. Under torture, the rebels accused one another of plotting the uprising. Tiradentes was the only one who refused to betray his companions. He insisted: "I am the only one responsible."

At their trial, Tiradentes argued passionately for the cause of freedom. He and his followers were convicted, however. All but Tiradentes were forced to leave the country. The Tooth Puller was sentenced to death. At dawn on April 21, 1792, Tiradentes walked to the gallows, drums beating, the town crier calling out his name through the streets. He was hanged and beheaded, and his head was stuck on a pole as a warning to others.

Although Tiradentes was killed, his bravery inspired many other colonists. Brazil finally won independence in 1822. April 21 is now a national holiday, called Tiradentes Day. The freedom fighter's hometown was renamed Tiradentes in his honor. And today almost every town in Brazil has its Tiradentes Street or Square.

A Vast Country

Brazil is the fifth largest country in the world. It dominates the South American continent, sharing borders with every

A 125-foot (38-meter)-tall statue of Christ watches over Rio de Janeiro from the top of Corcovado Mountain.

other country except Chile and Ecuador. Along its eastern side Brazil faces the Atlantic Ocean. The sea gives the country its beautiful beaches and the longest unbroken coastline in the world.

Brazil has five main regions, which are so different from one another that they are almost like different countries.

The Northeast: Birthplace of Brazilian Culture

The northeast is the part of Brazil that bulges out into the Atlantic Ocean. When the Portuguese first came to Brazil, this is where they settled. This is also where they met the native Indians and brought slaves from Africa. The special blend of Indian, Portuguese, and African customs created modern Brazil.

The northeast is the poorest part of Brazil. A narrow, fertile strip of land runs along the coast from the city of Natal to the state of Bahia. Cacao and sugarcane grow here, and beaches attract tourists. But beyond this 150-mile (241-kilometer)-wide area, the land is rocky and dry. Sometimes rain doesn't fall for years. When it does, it often comes in sudden storms, flooding the land. Millions of people have moved to the south to escape the difficult life in the northeast.

The largest city in the northeast is Salvador. It is known for its many churches. About two hundred churches can be found in this old city.

The North: Land of the Mighty Amazon

The north covers half of Brazil, but not many people live in this region. It lies almost entirely within the Amazon Basin and is covered by the world's largest tropical rain forest.

The Amazon Basin takes its name from the Amazon River, the second-longest river in the world. The Amazon is so deep that oceangoing ships can sail over 2,000 miles (3,218 kilometers) upriver. In some places, the Amazon is so wide that you can't see from one side to the other. The mouth of the river—the place where it meets the Atlantic Ocean—is huge: about 205 miles (330 kilometers) wide. In the middle of the river's mouth is an island, Marajó, which is larger than the country of Switzerland.

Vessels as large as oceangoing ships and as small as this dugout canoe use the Amazon River as an aquatic highway.

The rain forest in the Amazon Basin is one of the wettest places on earth. Scientists estimate that millions of different kinds of plants and animals live in the hot, steamy forest. If you walked through the rain forest, you would see familiar animals such as parrots, hummingbirds, hawks, turtles, alligators, snakes, and monkeys. You might also see some animals you have never heard of.

The capybara (kap-ih-BAH-rah), which looks like a large guinea pig, is the world's largest rodent: It can weigh as much as 150 pounds (68 kilograms) and grow as long as 5 feet (1.5 meters). It can be found swimming in the river, paddling along with its eyes just above the water.

Then there is the piranha, a meat-eating fish, and the anaconda, the largest snake in the world. They share the waters of the Amazon with the electric eel, which stuns its victims with an electric shock.

Other unusual creatures include the morpho, a butterfly that has a wingspan of up to seven inches (eighteen centimeters) across, larger than that of some birds. There are also bird-eating spiders as big as a fist, and tiny tree frogs the size of a thumbnail.

With so many kinds of living things, the rain forest is alive with chirps, clicks, hums, buzzes, and dozens of other sounds.

The West Central: Brasília, the Nation's Capital

Until the 1960s, the west central region had no roads and few people. Today it is the fastest-growing part of Brazil. This is

Emperor tamarin

Peanut bug

Eyelash viper

The Amazon Basin is home to some of the strangest—and most beautiful— animals on earth.

because Brasília, the nation's capital, was built there in the 1950s. The place for the capital city was chosen to encourage people to settle in the interior of the country.

Workers cut a highway through the wilderness, flew materials in by plane, and built a modern city of marble, glass, and steel. To show the Indian heritage of Brazil, the city's designers arranged the buildings in the form of a bow and arrow. Brazilian government offices, the University of Brasília, and the National Theater are in the capital city.

The Southeast: São Paulo and Rio de Janeiro

East of Brasília, a steep ridge of mountains slopes down to a narrow plain along the Atlantic coast. Most Brazilians live in this fertile region.

São Paulo (sow-PAW-loo), the largest city in Brazil, is located here. It is a bustling city with more than eleven million people—the third-largest city in the world. São Paulo is the industrial center of Brazil.

Rio de Janeiro (REA-oh day jah-nair-oh) is the second-largest city in Brazil and one of the most beautiful cities in the world. Sugarloaf Mountain towers over the city on Guanabara Bay. Another mountain, Corcovado, is crowned by a statue of Christ with arms spread to welcome everyone to the city. People come from all over the world to play on Rio's beaches.

The South: Cowboys and Waterfalls

Southern Brazil is the smallest of the five regions. On wide, open prairies, Brazilian cowboys called gaúchos (gah-OOH-shoo) raise cattle. The largest city in this region is Pôrto Alegre.

To the west, on the border between Brazil, Paraguay, and Argentina, a magnificent semicircle of 275 waterfalls rises out

Gaúchos may look colorful and romantic, but raising cattle is hard, dusty work.

of the jungle. They are called the Iguaçú Falls, which means "great waters" in the Tupí-Guaraní Indian language. The falls stretch over a 3-mile (4.8-kilometer) area. With their crashing waters, fine mists, and beautiful rainbows, the Iguaçú Falls are a popular place for tourists to visit.

Christmas in Summer

Since Brazil lies south of the equator, seasons there are opposite those of the United States: Summer is from December to March, and winter is from June to September. So in Brazil, Christmas and New Year's are good times to go to the beach!

The First People in Brazil

The first people in Brazil came from Asia about ten thousand years ago. They walked across a strip of land that once connected Russia and Alaska, and made their way south. Little is known of the history of these first people, or Indians, other than that they lived by hunting, fishing, and raising crops.

In 1500 the explorer Pedro Alvares Cabral sailed from Portugal and landed in northeastern Brazil. According to legend, he had meant to sail to India, but stormy winds blew his ships across the Atlantic Ocean. Cabral thought Brazil was a small island and never knew he had come upon a continent.

In 1530 some Portuguese settled in the northeastern part of the country. They found a certain tree there that produced red and purple dyes, colors that were popular in Europe. The tree was called *pau-brasil* (POW-brah-ZEEL), or brazilwood. The Portuguese settlers did a lively business in the wood. Soon the country became known as Land of the Brazilwood. Later, the name was shortened to Brazil.

After a while, the settlers found that they had cut down most of the brazilwood trees. Then they began to raise sugarcane. At first they forced the Indians to work as slaves on the sugarcane plantations. But, because of the harsh conditions, many native people died or ran away. So, over the next two

In this Brazilian scene painted in 1649, a man on horseback directs slaves.

hundred years, the Portuguese brought millions of Africans to work as slaves. First they worked on the sugarcane plantations. Later they were put to work on cotton and tobacco plantations.

In the late 1500s two groups of people explored the interior of Brazil. One was the missionaries, who wanted to teach Christianity to the Indians. The other group was called the *bandeirantes* (bahn-day-RAHN-chees), which means "flag carriers." The *bandeirantes* hunted for gold and for Indians to enslave. They were known as cruel slave hunters, but also as pioneers who cut through the forests and expanded Brazil's borders.

Gold and Diamonds

In the 1690s adventurers discovered gold and diamonds in Brazil's interior. Thousands of people rushed to what is now the state of Minas Gerais, which means "general mines." Between 1700 and 1800, tons of gold and millions of diamonds were mined.

The newly wealthy rode in gold carriages, wore clothes made with golden thread, and threw nuggets of gold at the feet of visiting performers. Artists and architects from Portugal built ornate churches and government buildings.

The boom in gold and diamonds was followed by the discovery of an even more important source of wealth—coffee. With its cool climate and rich soil, southern Brazil became a coffee-growing center. Today, Brazil still produces more coffee and sugar than any other country in the world.

A King and Two Emperors

In 1808 King João (zhuh-AW) VI of Portugal moved his court to Brazil because of fighting in Europe. He ruled until 1821 and then returned to Portugal, leaving his son Pedro in command.

For a number of years some Brazilian patriots, like Tiradentes, had been trying to free the nation from Portuguese rule.

Pedro had grown up in Brazil and felt more loyal to it than to Portugal. On September 7, 1822, Pedro raised his sword on the banks of the Ipiranga River and shouted, "Independence or death!" He proclaimed Brazil an independent country and named himself emperor, Pedro I.

RUBBER MONEY

In the late 1800s rubber made Brazil rich. Cars had just been invented, and people around the world wanted rubber for tires. At that time Brazil was the only country that had many rubber trees, which grew in the Amazon Basin.

Thanks to rubber, Manaus became the wealthiest city in South America around 1900. Although it was in the heart of the Amazon Basin, Manaus had electric lights before London did. Ships brought beautiful doors and staircases from Italy to adorn the homes of the wealthy. A seven-hundred-seat opera house was built, modeled after the Grand Opéra in Paris. Some rubber barons were so wealthy—and extravagant—that they sent their laundry to Paris to be washed!

In 1914 the boom ended. Rubber trees were being cultivated in Southeast Asia, and Brazil was no longer the only source of rubber.

Some of the world's most famous artists danced and sang at the Manaus Opera House, the five-million-dollar "opera in the jungle."

Pedro II, whose reign ended in 1889, was the last emperor of Brazil.

In 1840, at the age of fourteen, Pedro II became the second emperor. He was a popular ruler who knew fourteen languages and encouraged education and the development of the country. Once he said, "If I were not emperor, I should like to be a schoolteacher." He ruled Brazil for nearly fifty years.

Pedro II wanted to end slavery, and in 1888 the "Golden Law" was passed, freeing all slaves. Both the wealthy landowners and military leaders did not like Pedro II's policies. In 1889 he was overthrown and a republic was established.

Presidents, Dictators, and Generals

During the past one hundred years, Brazilians have had different ideas about how to end poverty. Landownership is a major problem. A few wealthy people own most of the land, while most people own no land and are poor. There have been many arguments between those who think the land should be shared and those who don't.

Partly as a result of these troubles, the military has overthrown the elected government many times. From 1889 to 1930 there were thirteen presidents. From 1930 to 1945 and from 1951 to 1954 Brazil was ruled by a dictator, Getúlio Vargas.

João Goulart, who became president in 1961, supported taking some land from the rich to give to the poor. The military leaders and wealthy landowners did not like Goulart's plans. With the help of the United States, they overthrew him in 1964.

For the next twenty years, Brazil was run by generals.

Newspapers were censored and political debate was not allowed. People who criticized the government were often jailed, tortured, and sometimes killed.

At first the economy grew while the military ruled the country. Superhighways, dams, and nuclear power plants were built. But Brazil fell deeply into debt as the government borrowed billions of dollars from foreign banks to pay for the development projects. When Brazil's economy weakened in the 1980s, people called for a new government. Rule by the military was ended, and in 1989 Brazilians voted in a direct presidential election. It was the first one in twenty-nine years. Today, Fernando Henrique Cardoso is president. He faces the challenge of meeting the needs of all the people—the rich and the poor, city dwellers and farmers, Indians and the many other peoples who make up the great land of Brazil.

BRAZILIAN GOVERNMENT

Brazil is a federal republic. The head of government is the president, who holds office for five years and cannot be reelected. Congress is made up of the Senate, with 81 members, and the Chamber of Deputies, with 503 members. Senators serve for eight years; deputies serve for four years. The Supreme Court is the highest court in the country. It has 11 justices, who are appointed by the president with the Senate's approval.

Brazil has twenty-six states, plus the Federal District. The states and the Federal District each have a lawmaking assembly and a governor.

The ancestors of Brazil's Indian people came to South America from Asia about thirty thousand years ago.

2

Indian, Portuguese, and African Roots

The Brazilians are a blend of many peoples. Their roots can be traced to the Indians, the Portuguese settlers, and the African slaves. Later, in the late 1800s, millions of people came from Italy, Lebanon, Germany, Spain, Japan, and other countries to find work. Over time, many of these different groups blended to form the modern nation of Brazil.

Sacred Places in the Forest

Of all the people in Brazil, perhaps the most distinctive group is the Indians, the original inhabitants of the land.

About 100,000 Indians are left today. There were between two to five million when the Portuguese arrived. Thousands died from diseases, such as smallpox and measles, that they caught from the Portuguese. Others were killed by the new-comers.

Some Indians live deep in the rain forest and follow their traditional ways. They hunt animals with bows and arrows, and catch fish using nets, traps, or bows and arrows. Some tribes live in large community houses, while others live in

21

Using a blowgun that shoots poisoned darts, a hunter can kill an animal as large and fierce as a jaguar.

small, individual family houses. Besides finding nuts, berries, and honey in the forest, they grow crops like bananas, corn, and tobacco.

The forest is a sacred place for the Indians, who believe that every living thing has a spirit. They know which trees and plants are good for food and medicine. But the Indians take only what they need to survive.

Though some Indians still follow the old ways, most have had contact with people of European background. Since the 1960s, the Brazilian government has encouraged people from the overcrowded cities to move into the forest. Unfortunately, the new people destroyed great areas of trees and fought with the Indians. Life has completely changed for many Indians. Many now live in permanent villages, wear clothes, and use radios and rifles instead of bows and arrows. Some live in special areas, called reservations, that the government has set aside for them.

Indians in Brazil were not considered full citizens until 1988. Today, many speak out for their rights. They say that the forest is theirs and that others should stop cutting it down.

An Indian man attends a protest against building hydroelectric dams on the Amazon River.

The Only Portuguese-Speaking Country in South America

Almost all Brazilians speak Portuguese, a language that comes from Latin and is related to Spanish, French, and Italian. Brazil is the only country in South America where Portuguese is the official language.

The Portuguese spoken in Brazil is different from that spoken in Portugal. This is partly because some twenty thousand Indian words have become part of Brazilian Portuguese. Words such as *samba*, which come from African languages, have also added to the richness of Brazilian Portuguese.

Although Portuguese is the language of everyday life for most Brazilians, Indian languages are spoken in the remote areas of the country.

Catholics and Spirit Believers

Most Brazilians are Roman Catholic. There are thousands of churches throughout Brazil. Many were built when the Portuguese first brought Catholicism to Brazil. One, the São Francisco Church and Convent in Salvador, is elaborately carved and covered with gold on the inside. Other churches are supermodern, such as the cathedral in Brasília. Brazil also has many Protestants, as well as smaller numbers of Mormons, Jews, Muslims, and Buddhists.

Next to Catholicism, the most widespread religion in Brazil is *candomblé* (kan-dom-BLEH), which was brought to Brazil by African slaves. Because the slaves were not allowed to practice their religion, they gave Christian names to their gods. The *candomblé* god of the harvest, Oxalá, was associated with Jesus. Iemanjá (ee-ay-mawn-ZHUH), the goddess of the sea, was associated with Mary. Today about one-third of all

The many beautiful churches in Brazil range in age from hundreds of years old to brand-new.

Brazilians, including people of all races and many who also consider themselves Catholic, participate in *candomblé* ceremonies.

SAY IT IN PORTUGUESE

Good morning	*Bom dia* (bong GEE-ya)
Good night	*Boa noite* (bwa NOY-chee)
Good-bye	*Adeus* (ah-DEH-oos)
How are you?	*Como vai?* (COH-moo vai)
Is everything okay?	*Tudo bem?* (too-doo bang)
Fine, great!	*Tudo bem!* (too-doo bang)
Let's go	*Vamos embora* (VAH-moose eng-BOH-rah)
Excuse me	*Desculpe* (desh-CUL-pee)
Yes	*Sim* (seem)
No	*Não* (now)
Please	*Faz favor* (fahz fah-VOHR)
Thank you	*Obrigado* (oh-bree-GAH-doo)—males
	Obrigada (oh-bree-GAH-dah)—females

FROM TUPÍ-GUARANÍ TO ENGLISH

Today many Indian words have become part of the everyday language of Portuguese-speaking Brazilians. That's not surprising, but did you know that many Indian words have come into the English language as well? For example, *cashew*, *cougar*, *jaguar*, *piranha*, *tapioca*, and *toucan* are all Tupí-Guaraní Indian words.

People who follow *candomblé* believe that their priests and priestesses can contact the gods, called *orixás* (oh-ree-SHAS), and people who have died. In their ceremonies people chant songs and dance to drums until the priestess goes into a trance and feels the spirit of the god or dead person. These spirits are asked to cure the sick or help people in other ways. The city of Salvador, in the state of Bahia, is especially known for its many houses of *candomblé*.

Earning a Living in Brazil

Some areas of Brazil are modern and up to date. People work in high-rise offices and use computers and the latest technology.

At a candomblé *ceremony in São Paulo, people seek help from ancestors and spirit messengers.*

27

In other areas people fish and hunt, raise crops, or struggle just to live.

Some Brazilians have very good jobs, but others earn barely enough money to support themselves. Almost one out of every five Brazilians does not have a job. Many others find temporary work such as protecting cars from thieves, delivering groceries, or walking dogs. It is estimated that seven out of ten Brazilians live in poverty. The poorest are women, blacks, and Indians.

Farmers travel to work in a cart pulled by oxen.

Two Brazils: Poor and Rich

The rich and the poor in Brazil seem to live in different worlds. The wealthy and the middle class live in modern houses or apartments and own cars. Children in these families go to school, have plenty to eat, and take vacations with their parents. Most of these families have maids who cook and clean for them.

About half of all Brazilians live in slums. In these slums, called *favelas* (fah-VEL-ahs), people live in shacks made of tin, cardboard, or scraps of wood. Many lack running water. The people usually don't have enough food to eat. When they get sick, they cannot afford a doctor. In the countryside, too, houses often have no running water or electricity. The

The word favela *may come from another word meaning "honeycomb." The people in this Rio* favela *are certainly as crowded as bees in a hive.*

villagers have to go to the river to do their washing or to get drinking water.

Many poor children in Brazil are homeless.

Thousands of Brazilian children are orphans. Their parents have either died or abandoned them. The young people live and sleep in the streets, begging, stealing, or working to get money for food. Sometimes they shine shoes or carry bags of groceries to earn money. They don't have a chance to go to school.

The contrast between the rich and the poor in Brazil is so sharp that in some cities the *favela* is right across the street from an expensive hotel. Some Brazilians wear designer clothes and drive expensive cars, while others wear rags and beg for something to eat.

Baggy Pants and Turbans

Most Brazilians wear Western-style clothes, like jeans and T-shirts or suits and dresses. In certain areas of the country, though, the people have their own special clothes. In the northeast, where many people of African descent live, the women wear pleated white dresses, colorful turbans, and beaded necklaces and bracelets. In the south gaúchos wear baggy pants tucked into leather boots, wide hats, and bandannas around their necks. And some Indian tribes in the hot rain forest wear no clothes at all—though many paint their bodies red and black with dyes made from the juice of plants, and wear jewelry made from beads and feathers.

People of African descent have been living in Brazil for almost five hundred years.

Many places hold carnivals during the week before Lent, but Rio de Janeiro is famous for its elaborate costumes and parades.

3

The Brazilian Way of Life

The family is the center of life in Brazil. Families are usually big: Many have between five and ten children. Some families have as many as twenty children!

Brazilians stay in close touch with their extended family—grandparents, uncles, aunts, and cousins. Even distant cousins see each other often. Baptisms, weddings, and funerals are big family events attended by hundreds of people.

The father is the head of the family. Usually the father works and earns money, and the mother raises the children and takes care of the

Families in Brazil are often large, warm, and closely knit.

house. But in many middle-class and poor families, women and young people work to help support their families.

There used to be a saying in Brazil that a woman should leave home only for her baptism, marriage, and funeral. But in Brazil today, women vote, have legal rights, and work in government, the arts, and other careers. Men, however, still dominate life in Brazil.

Mansions, Stilts, and Floating Houses

Brazilians live in many different kinds of houses. In the rain forest some people live in thatched houses made from palm tree leaves. Near the banks of the Amazon River, wooden houses are built on stilts so they stay dry when the river rises. Some houses are built like rafts so that they float. In some areas you can find floating stores, churches, and gasoline stations!

In big cities, high-rise apartments made of steel and concrete are within view of the *favelas,* with their tin and cardboard shacks. Some wealthy people live in large, beautiful houses. In these mansions rooms open onto patios or courtyards with trees and flowers. Few families in Brazil have dishwashers, washing machines, or other labor-saving machines. Most people who can afford to do so hire servants to clean their homes and prepare their meals.

Carnival Time!

The biggest, most famous festival in Brazil is Carnival, which marks the last few days before Lent, in February or March. Everything stops for four days and nights as people dress up in elaborate costumes of feathers, stars, swirling skirts, and headdresses, and dance in the streets all night long. Other people go to fancy costume balls and parties. Children, too, dress up in costumes, paint their faces, and dance for hours at parties.

One of the biggest attractions of Carnival is the parade of

The water rises so high during the rainy season that houses along the Amazon River must be built on stilts.

The homes of the wealthy are often brightly colored and intricately decorated.

the samba schools. Named after a Brazilian dance, samba schools are neighborhood groups that spend months making fancy costumes, decorating floats, and practicing songs, skits, and dances that tell stories from Brazilian history or folklore.

During Carnival in Rio de Janeiro, the members of the samba schools sing and dance around the floats in huge parades through the streets. People come from all over the world to see the big parades held in Rio.

Goddess of the Sea

Another festival is the Feast of Iemanjá, a religious tradition that began in Africa. On New Year's Eve on the beaches of Rio, people light hundreds of candles and set them on white lace

The streets of Belo Horizonte, a city in east Brazil, are filled with color and noise at Carnival time.

cloths at the edge of the water. Dressed in white, the people dance, sing, and offer gifts of fruit, perfume, and flowers to Iemanjá, the goddess of the sea. They give thanks for the past year and ask the goddess for blessings for the coming year.

At midnight everyone throws gifts into the water. If the gifts are washed away to sea, the giver believes, the new year will be good.

Balloons and Bonfires

Since most Brazilians are Catholic, traditional Christian holidays are celebrated. During Holy Week, which ends with Easter Sunday, processions and celebrations are held throughout the country. Families go to church, and children play with Easter eggs and eat chocolate.

Saint days, which are named after Catholic saints, are also important holidays. Since the saint days of Saint Anthony, Saint

John, and Saint Peter are all in June, Brazilians celebrate two weeks of parties called the June Festivals. The sky is lit up by bonfires, miniature hot-air balloons with candles in them, and fireworks. People have parties and dance until late at night.

Saint Anthony's Day is June 13. Since Saint Anthony is the patron of young women in search of a husband, unmarried girls often wear white veils to church and pray for a good husband. Sometimes they drop candle wax into a glass of water to find out what kind of work their future husband will do. If the wax takes the shape of an airplane, for example, then they believe they will marry a man who will be a pilot.

Another custom is for girls to write the names of boys they know on pieces of paper and put the papers under their pillows. The name they pull out is said to be that of the boy they will marry.

On Saint John's Day, June 24, young people throughout the land dress in clothes typical of the interior of Brazil. Girls wear flowered skirts, white blouses, and large straw hats, and boys dress in pants with suspenders and plaid shirts. They dance around bonfires that burn all night. Some people say that couples who hold hands and jump over the bonfire at midnight will be lifelong friends.

One of the biggest bonfires in Brazil is in Osasco, a town near São Paulo. It burns for the whole last week of June. During this week, Saint Peter's Day is celebrated with fireworks and dancing.

The Statue in the Water

The saint day of Our Lady of Aparecida (Nossa Senhora de Aparecida), the patron saint of Brazil, is October 12. This day celebrates a miracle that was said to occur in October 1717.

During the June Festivals, people celebrate till late at night all along the beach.

One day, according to the story, the Portuguese governor stopped at a fisherman's cottage and demanded a meal. The fisherman and two friends hurried to their boat to go fishing, but they had no luck. So they prayed. When they threw their nets into the water again, they pulled out a two-foot (seven-meter)-high statue of the Virgin Mary. Then they caught so many fish that their nets nearly burst.

Every year millions of pilgrims visit the church built to house the statue.

Father Christmas

Christmas, or Natal (na-TAHL), is celebrated with church services, songs, and presents. Many people decorate their homes with a manger and a Christmas tree. People often plant the tree in a giant flowerpot and use it from year to year.

Christmas Eve supper is a special meal of turkey or ham,

sweets, and nuts. A favorite dessert is rabanadas (hah-bah-NAH-dahs), bread soaked in sugar, cinnamon, and wine and fried, like French toast. After supper, children wait for Father Christmas (Papai Noel; pah-PIE noh-ELL). They believe that he enters homes through a window and leaves presents in shoes placed on the windowsill or on the floor.

Eating the Brazilian Way

Mealtimes are family times in Brazil. The whole family eats together whenever possible.

Breakfast, or *café-da-manhã* (kah-FEH-dah-mahn-YAH), is usually a light meal of coffee with hot milk (*café com leite*; kah-FEH kong LAY-chee), buttered bread, and sometimes fruit.

Lunch, or *almoço* (ahl-MOH-soo), is the biggest meal of the day—and often lasts for two hours. Served at noon, it may include rice, beans, salad, meat, or other dishes, depending on what people can afford. The poor often have a simple meal of rice, black beans, and manioc (MAN-ee-ock). Manioc is a root vegetable that can be eaten by itself or made into flour. Working people often go home to have lunch with their families.

Dinner, or *jantar* (zhahn-TAHR), is a light meal of chicken or fish, salad, and dessert eaten around seven-thirty or eight-thirty in the evening. Some people also have a midmorning and midafternoon snack of coffee with cookies or bread.

Every region in Brazil has its own special dishes. In the northeast food has an African flavor. One of the most popular dishes is vatapá (vah-tah-PAH), which is made of shrimp, fish, and coconut milk. In the Amazon area two favorite dishes are duck in a rich sauce, called pato no tucupí (PAH-toh noh too-koo-PEE), and tacacá (tah-kah-KAH), a thick yellow soup with shrimp and garlic.

This woman is on her way to market with a basketful of produce. Brazil grows many kinds of tropical fruits and vegetables.

In the south people like to eat churrasco (shoo-HAHS-koo), chunks of meat roasted over hot coals and served with rice, fried corn mush, and sometimes a fried banana. This dish was first eaten by Brazilian cowboys who roasted meat over an open fire on the southern plains. Today it can be ordered in restaurants in many parts of Brazil.

One dish popular everywhere is the national dish, feijoada (fay-ZHWAH-dah). This is a thick stew of pork and black beans served with white rice and manioc flour, kale (a dark green, leafy vegetable), and orange slices. The ears, tail, feet, and even the snout of a pig used to be included in the feijoada, though they are often left out today. Brazilians traditionally eat feijoada on Saturday afternoons.

Red Bananas and Strong Coffee

With its tropical climate, Brazil has hundreds of kinds of fruit. Pineapple, melons, apples, oranges, peaches, and strawberries are common. There are also many kinds of bananas—red bananas, purple bananas, and green bananas!

And there are tropical fruits: papayas, mangoes, persim-

CHOCOLATE BALLS ("BRIGADEIROS")

1 can sweetened condensed milk (12 ounces)
4 tablespoons chocolate powder (unsweetened cocoa)
1 tablespoon butter or margarine
1/4 teaspoon salt
1 cup chocolate sprinkles

In a medium-sized pan, combine the condensed milk and chocolate powder. Cook over low temperature stirring constantly, until the mixture pulls away from the sides of the pan. Add butter and salt. Mix thoroughly before removing mixture from heat. When cool, make into little balls about 1 inch wide, and roll them in the chocolate sprinkles.

To serve, place in small paper baking cups. Makes 20 balls.

---

mons, *cajú* (which has a cashew nut inside), guavas (a yellow pear-shaped fruit), and jaboticaba (a red or black berry used to make jelly or pie). Another fruit, used in making a popular soft drink, is the *guaraná* (gwah-rah-NAH), a berry.

Coffee is Brazil's national drink. Brazilians like to drink "little coffees" (*cafezinhos*; kah-feh-ZEE-nyoo) throughout the day. *Cafezinho* is very strong coffee served in small cups with lots of sugar. Sometimes up to half the cup is filled with sugar before the coffee is poured in. Children drink coffee with breakfast and after meals, just like adults.

Besides delicious foods from their own country, Brazilians also eat food from all over the world. A Brazilian child might eat hamburgers and french fries at McDonald's, spaghetti at an Italian restaurant, or rice and vegetables at a Japanese restaurant.

In the foods they eat, Brazilians bring together many traditions—and enjoy them all.

Even children of kindergarten age wear school uniforms.

4

SCHOOL AND RECREATION

Learning and Playing in Brazil

Brazilian children between the ages of seven and fourteen are supposed to go to school, but not all do. Some must work to earn money for food. Others live in the countryside far away from the nearest school. Even those who go to school don't go for very long. Fewer than half the teenagers in Brazil go to high school.

Many schools are overcrowded and don't have enough teachers, books, or desks. Some parents pay to send their children to private schools, which usually have better teachers, libraries, and gyms than public schools.

The Brazilian government is trying to help more children go to school. It has built new schools with modern equipment. Free lunches are provided for poor children. Also, children who work can now attend classes in the evenings.

Morning School and Afternoon School

Elementary school, called First Degree (*Primeiro Grau*; pree-MAY-ruh graw), begins at age seven and lasts for eight years. In most schools children must wear a uniform. Boys usually

Eighty out of every hundred Brazilians know how to read and write by the time they grow up.

wear white shirts and dark blue pants, and girls often wear white blouses and pleated blue skirts. Both boys and girls wear black shoes.

Children go to school from March to the middle of December. Because there are so many children and so few schools and teachers, some children go to school in the morning and some in the afternoon. The morning group goes from about seven to eleven-thirty, and the afternoon group from one to five-thirty. This way the same school can teach twice as many children.

For the first four years, children have one teacher for all subjects. From fifth grade on, different teachers teach different subjects. Each class lasts about fifty minutes. A fifth grader might take math, social studies, Portuguese, English, gym, and science. Children also get time to play outside. One favorite game is *rela-rela* (HEH-lah-HEH-lah), or tag.

High school, or Second Degree (*Segundo Grau*; sih-GOON-doo grouw), is for three years, from age fifteen to eighteen. Students who finish high school can go to one of the ninety-three universities in Brazil, such as the University of Rio de Janeiro. Or they can attend a technical school, where they study such subjects as computer science or engineering.

Not many young people are fortunate enough to go on to college. This is partly because there aren't enough spaces in college for all those who want to go, and partly because so many drop out of school at a young age. But some students want so much to go to college that they take the vestibular, a hard exam required for college. They may take it again and again until they are successful—even if it takes four or five years to pass the test.

Crazy About Soccer

When Brazilian children aren't in school or working, they love to play soccer. Called *futebol* (foo-tih-BAWL), soccer is the single most popular sport in Brazil. Every school, town, and city has a soccer field. Some fields are huge stadiums, like the Maracanã in Rio de Janeiro, which is the biggest in the world. Others are as simple as an empty lot in a town, or a clearing in the forest.

The first gift a Brazilian boy receives is usually a soccer ball. By the time he's eight, he knows how to kick, dribble, and handle the ball with his feet. Every chance they get, Brazilian boys pick up a soccer ball and kick it around. They dream of joining a junior league team and going on to play professionally. Every boy hopes he'll be the one to make the winning play in the big championships.

With millions of players and twenty thousand teams,

hundreds of soccer matches are held in Brazil each year. The best Brazilian players compete in matches with teams from nearby countries to see which country's team is the best in that region. Then the best regional teams compete in the biggest championship of all, the World Cup.

When Brazil plays in the World Cup, stores and banks close and the whole country watches the game. If Brazil wins, people celebrate all night long, waving flags and dancing in the streets.

In 1994 Brazil won the World Cup championship—for the fourth time. Brazilians are proud that their country is the first ever to win four World Cup championships. Romário and

People pack Rio's huge Maracanã Stadium to watch soccer matches.

THE BEST SOCCER PLAYER OF ALL TIME

Perhaps the greatest soccer player of all time is the Brazilian Pelé, whose real name is Edson Arantes do Nascimento. Pelé started playing when he was just fifteen years old. During his eighteen-year career, he scored more than 1,200 goals and led Brazil to three World Cup championships. Once when Pelé was playing in Africa, two countries that were at war declared a three-day peace so they could watch him play.

After he retired in 1974 Pelé came to the United States and played with the New York Cosmos. Today he is minister of sports in the Brazilian government. Thanks to Pelé, young people around the world have been inspired to play soccer.

In Brazil, Pelé is sometimes called Perola Negra–Black Pearl.

Bebeto are famous players who helped Brazil win the 1994 World Cup.

Race Cars and Volleyball

Car racing is also a popular sport in Brazil. Millions of people watch the worldwide races on television, and a Brazilian Grand Prix race is held every year in São Paulo or Rio de Janeiro. Brazilians Nelson Piquet and Ayrton Senna won many international racing championships.

Volleyball is popular with both men and women. A Brazilian women's team won the World Cup in volleyball in 1991, and a men's team won a gold medal at the Olympics in 1992. Basketball, too, is well liked, and Brazil has twice won the men's world championships. But Brazilians don't have to win a prize to enjoy volleyball or basketball: They like to play these games just for fun at schools and clubs, or at the beach.

Sand, Sun, and Water

Brazilians love the beach. They go there on weekends, for vacations—and whenever else they can. People in Rio de Janeiro spend so much time at the beach that they call it their living room!

At the beach, people swim and sunbathe, but they also play soccer and volleyball, surf, jog, or exercise. And there's plenty to eat. Food stands sell snacks, restaurants sell seafood, and fruit sellers carry around pineapples or coconuts, which they slice open with knives. Small boys sell tropical fruit ice pops called *picolés* (pee-koh-LEHS). Other people sell soft drinks, ice cream, hats, tanning lotion, kites, and mats to lie on.

During the summer months, the beach is always crowded. For people who live along the coast, the beach is an important meeting place. Children do homework there, business executives make deals, and friends meet. Others dance, pray, play music—or simply enjoy the sun.

Sports Clubs and Soap Operas

Sports clubs are popular for those who can afford them. They're especially popular where no beach is available, such as in the interior of Brazil. People gather at the clubs to swim, play soccer or tennis, and have a good time.

In the evenings both children and adults like to watch television, especially soap operas, called *novelas*. Brazilians also love to watch soccer or car racing on television. Some people say television is now as popular as soccer, the beach, and music.

Whatever they're doing—whether it's going to school,

playing sports, or making music and dancing—Brazilians do it with spirit.

People come from all over the world to play and swim at Copacabana Beach.

49

African, Portuguese, Indian, and European influences mix to create a rhythm that is uniquely Brazilian.

5

Brazilian Treasures

Through their music, dance, literature, painting, and crafts, Brazilians celebrate life, history, and the special blend of customs that makes them who they are.

Samba Time

The samba is both a kind of music and a dance. Brazil is known all over the world for this popular musical style. A swaying, rhythmic dance, the samba is the heartbeat of Carnival. Some people say that the samba came from a mixture of Portuguese courtly songs, African rhythms, and native Indian footwork. Others say the samba came from the *batuque,* a kind of African music based on drums and hand clapping.

Bossa nova, which means "new beat," is a mixture of samba and American jazz. Its catchy sound became popular in the 1960s. "The Girl from Ipanema," written by Tom Jobim and the poet Vinicius de Moraes, is a bossa nova hit known around the world.

Brazil is also known for its classical music. Heitor Villa-Lobos is the country's most famous composer of classical music. In his operas and symphonies, he created a new sound that combined Brazilian folk melodies with classical orchestra music.

Capoeira: **The Fighting Dance**

Capoeira (kah-pooh-AY-rah) is a dance found only in Brazil. It looks like fighting, but the participants never touch. *Capoeira* started in the northeast in colonial times when masters punished slaves caught fighting. The slaves thought that this treatment was unfair, so they disguised the fighting with music and dance.

While two slaves fought, another played the *berimbau* (beh-reem-BOW), a bow-shaped musical instrument with a metal wire attached to a gourd at the bottom. The player shook the bow, rattling seeds in the gourd, and struck the wire with a copper coin. The slaves would kick and leap in perfect time with the twanging sound of the *berimbau*. If the master came, they continued but without hitting each other, so the master thought it was a dance.

Today *capoeira* is both a dance and a sport. It requires great skill, since participants can use only their legs, feet, heels, and heads—not their hands.

Dancers practicing the capoeira *must use great skill to avoid hitting each other.*

Paintings from the Earth

During the colonial period, most Brazilian art was of religious subjects and followed European art traditions. The outstanding artist of this period was Antônio Francisco Lisboa. He was better known, however, as Aleijadinho, or the Little Cripple.

The Last Supper *displays Aleijadinho's skill as a sculptor.*

Aleijadinho produced some of the finest sculptures in Brazil. When he was in his forties, Aleijadinho's hands became crippled by a disease. But he kept on sculpting for another thirty years by strapping a chisel and a mallet to his wrists.

In the nineteenth century, artists created new styles that reflected the tropical sun and bright colors of Brazil's landscape. In the twentieth century, perhaps the greatest Brazilian artist was Cândido Portinari. Raised on a coffee plantation in

BRAZILIAN WRITERS

Joaquim Maria Machado de Assís (1839–1908), composed his first poem, "To An Angel," when he was sixteen years old. At seventeen he worked for a printer, studying at night, while he wrote novels and poetry. He was one of Brazil's greatest novelists and wrote for almost fifty years.

Euclides da Cunha (1866–1909), was a journalist who wrote about the difficulties minorities faced in Brazil. One of his books, *Rebellion in the Backlands,* is about an uprising in Bahia in the 1890s. Da Cunha starts the book by showing the rebels as religious fanatics, but ends by showing the brutality of the army.

Mario de Andrade (1893–1945), was a poet and novelist. In his novel *Macunaima,* he tells the story of an Indian who moves to São Paulo and loses his cultural identity. Andrade traveled throughout the interior of Brazil. There he collected legends and folktales, which he included in his novel.

Clarice Lispector (1926–1977), became a lawyer, married, and published her first book all in the same year. Her books are about the inner world of characters trying to understand the meaning of life. Her novel *The Hour of the Star* was made into a movie.

Jorge Amado (1912–   ), is a leading novelist today. A popular storyteller, he writes about the lives of ordinary people. He describes fishermen, cacao plantation workers, and adventurers in the northeast region. *Gabriela: Clove and Cinnamon* is one of his best-known works. His books have been translated into many languages and made into movies.

the interior of Brazil, he painted the suffering of farmworkers. In some paintings he made their hands and feet very large, as though to suggest that was all they had.

Portinari liked to try out new ideas. Once he sent for sixty pounds (twenty-seven kilograms) of earth from different areas of Brazil, and mixed the black, purple, red, and yellow dirt in with his paints. Portinari was one of the first Brazilian artists

Cândido Portinari's painting of a coffee plantation shows farmhands hard at work.

to become world famous. Today his huge paintings decorate the walls at the United Nations in New York City and at the Library of Congress in Washington, D.C.

Buildings of Prayer

Brazilian architecture is admired worldwide. Some of the older cities, such as Ouro Prêto and Olinda, are considered world treasures by the United Nations. That is because they have so many beautiful Portuguese-style churches and monasteries.

The best-known examples of modern Brazilian architec-

The influence of Portuguese art and architecture is evident in the dazzling interiors of many churches.

ture are in the capital city, Brasília. The main public buildings were designed by architect Oscar Niemeyer. One of his most famous buildings is the Cathedral of Brasília. It has fingers of concrete reaching to the sky, as if the building itself is praying.

Wishing for Good Luck

Brazil has a rich tradition of folk art and crafts. Before the Portuguese came, the Indians made pottery, masks in animal shapes, hammocks, baskets, mats, and jewelry. The Portuguese brought lace making, wood carving, leather work, and goldsmithing. African traditions include weaving, jewelry, wood sculpture, and charms to ward off evil. The mix of native Indian, African, and Portuguese traditions has given Brazilian folk art its unique character.

Today, folk artists sell their handmade jewelry, pottery,

and other wares at *feiras,* or open-air markets. In the northern region sandscapes are popular. These are scenes, made of different-colored sand, placed inside a bottle. It takes patience and skill to dye the sand and trickle it into the bottle in just the right places.

Lucky charms made of wood, silver, or gems are popular throughout Brazil. One favorite charm is in the shape of a clenched fist, with the thumb sticking up between the first and second fingers. Many people wear this charm to ward off evil. But you must receive the charm as a gift. People say it won't work if you buy it for yourself.

From the drumbeat of the samba to the clicks and calls of the rain forest, Brazil is a fascinating land, one in which many traditions have blended to form a very special country.

Modern artists in Brazil paint lively pictures in bold colors.

Country Facts

Official Name: República Federativa do Brasil (Federal Republic of Brazil)

Capital: Brasília

Location: in South America, bordered on the east by the Atlantic Ocean; on the north, by French Guiana, Suriname, Guyana, Venezuela, Colombia; on the west, by Peru, Bolivia, Paraguay, Argentina; and on the south, by Uruguay

Area: 3,286,470 square miles (8,511,965 square kilometers). *Greatest distances:* east–west, 2,681 miles (4,314 kilometers); north–south, 2,731 miles (4,394 kilometers). *Coastline:* 4,578 miles (7,367 kilometers)

Elevation: *Highest:* Pico da Neblina, 9,889 feet (3,041 meters). *Lowest:* sea level

Climate: hot, with heavy rainfall, in the north; subtropical and dry, in the central plateau and the north; temperate in the south

Population: 150 million. *Distribution:* 75 percent live in cities on a narrow strip along the coast; 25 percent live in rural areas

Form of Government: federal republic

Important Products: *Agriculture:* coffee, sugar, soybeans, oranges, cotton, corn, beans, rice, manioc, wheat, potatoes, tobacco, bananas, peanuts, and cacao. *Industries:* autos and airplanes, communications, military equipment, and oil and fuel products. *Natural resources:* iron ore, manganese, bauxite, nickel, uranium, phosphates, tin, rubber, gold, platinum, crude oil, and timber

Basic Unit of Money: real; 1 real = 100 centavos

Language: Portuguese

Religion: 90 percent Roman Catholic; African-Brazilian religions (such as *candomblé*), Protestants, Mormons, Jews, Muslims, and Buddhists

Flag: green background with a yellow diamond in the center. On the diamond is a blue globe with 27 white stars. The stars represent Brazil's 26 states and the Federal District. A band across the globe gives the motto of Brazil: *Ordem e Progresso* ("Order and Progress").

National Anthem: *Hino Nacional* ("National Hymn")

Major Holidays: Feast Day of Iemanjá (New Year's Eve); New Year's Day; Carnival, the four days before Ash Wednesday; Good Friday, Friday before Easter; Easter; Tiradentes Day, April 21; Labor Day, May 1; Corpus Christi, in June; Independence Day, September 7; Our Lady of Aparecida Day, October 12; All Souls' Day, November 2; Proclamation of the Republic, November 15; Christmas

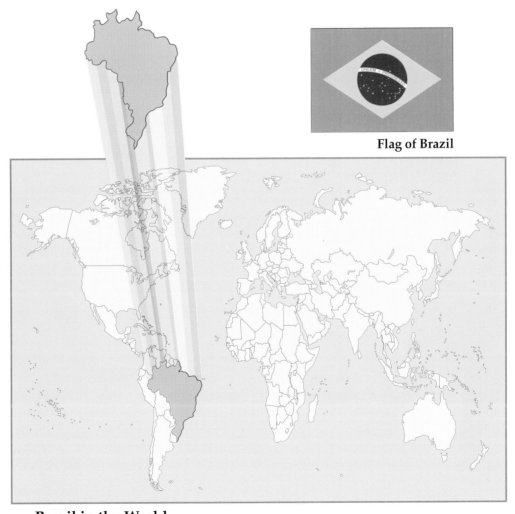

Flag of Brazil

Brazil in the World

Glossary

bandeirantes (bahn-day-RAHN-chees): "flag carriers"; people who explored the interior of Brazil while searching for gold and Indians to enslave

berimbau (beh-reem-BOW): musical instrument used in *capoeira* dance

bossa nova: music that mixes American jazz with Brazilian samba music

café com leite (kah-FEH kong LAY-chee): coffee with milk

candomblé (kan-dom-BLEH): African-Brazilian religion that combines Catholic and African beliefs

capoeira (kah-pooh-AY-rah): dance and sport, created by slaves, that looks like fighting; performed to instrument called *berimbau*

capybara (kap-ih-BAH-rah): world's largest rodent; looks like a large guinea pig

Carnival: festival of music, dancing, parades, costumes, and parties before Lent

churrasco (shoo-HAHS-koo): barbecued meat

favelas (fah-VEL-ahs): slums in Brazilian cities

feijoada (fay-ZHWAH-dah): Brazilian national dish, made of meat and black beans

futebol (foo-tih-BAWL): soccer

gaúcho (gah-OOH-shoo): cowboy of southern Brazil

Iemanjá (yeh-mawn-ZHAH): goddess of the sea in African-Brazilian religions

manioc (MAN-ee-ock): root vegetable that looks like a long potato and can be made into a flour used in breads, puddings, stews, and soup; also called cassava

novela: soap opera; most popular television shows in Brazil

orixás (oh-ree-SHAS): gods of African-Brazilian religions

Papai Noel (pah-PIE noh-ELL): Father Christmas

pau-brasil (POW-brah-ZEEL): brazilwood tree, which produces a red dye

samba: Brazilian music and dance

For Further Reading

Ang, Eng Tie. *Delightful Brazilian Cooking.* Seattle: Ambrosia Publications, 1993.

Arnold, Caroline. *Pele: The King of Soccer.* New York: Franklin Watts, 1992.

Bailey, Donna, and Anna Sproule. *Brazil: Where We Live.* Austin, Texas: Raintree Steck-Vaughn, 1990.

Christmas in Brazil. World Book Publications. Chicago: World Book, 1991.

Cobb, Vicki. *This Place Is Wet: The Brazilian Rain Forest.* New York: Walker, 1989.

Lewington, Anna. *Rain Forest Amerindians: Threatened Cultures.* Austin, Texas: Raintree Steck-Vaughn, 1993.

Lewington, Anna. *What Do We Know About the Amazonian Indians?* New York: Peter Bedrick Books, 1993.

Morrison, Marion. *Brazil: People and Places.* Parsippany, New Jersey: Silver Burdett, 1988.

Papi, Liza. *Carnavalia!: African-Brazilian Folklore and Crafts.* New York: Rizzoli International, 1994.

Waterlow, Julia. *The Amazon: Rivers of the World.* Austin, Texas: Raintree Steck-Vaughn, 1994.

Waterlow, Julia. *Brazil.* New York: Bookwright Press, 1992.

Index

Page numbers for illustrations are in boldface

About the Author

Irene Flum Galvin has been interested in Brazil ever since she heard the musical sound of the Portuguese language and the lilting melodies of Brazilian music. Her books for young readers include *The Maya of Central America* (Marshall Cavendish, 1996), *Japan: A Modern Land with Ancient Roots* (Marshall Cavendish, 1996), *Chile: Land of Poets and Patriots* (New York: Simon & Schuster/Dillon Books, 1990), and *The Rubber Band Boy* (New York State Council for Children, 1977), a picture book. Irene is the president of The Communications Connection, a writing and editorial services company in Rochester, New York, where she lives with her husband, Tom, and two children, Rachel and Danny.